Catholic Parish Administration

A HANDBOOK

Paul F. Peri

PAULIST PRESS
New York / Mahwah, NJ

The Scripture quotations contained herein are from the New Revised Standard Version: Catholic Edition Copyright © 1989 and 1993, by the Division of Christian Education of the National Council of the Churches of Christ in the United States of America. Used by permission. All rights reserved.

Cover images: Courtesy of Shutterstock.com
Cover design by Sharyn Banks
Book design by Lynn Else

Library of Congress Cataloging-in-Publication Data

Peri, Paul F.
    Catholic parish administration : a handbook / Paul F. Peri.
        p. cm.
    Includes bibliographical references (p.   ).
    ISBN 978-0-8091-4752-6 (alk. paper) — ISBN 978-1-61643-092-4
    1. Church management. 2. Catholic Church. I. Title.
    BV652.P48 2012
    254'.02—dc23

                                                        2011039427

Published by Paulist Press
997 Macarthur Boulevard
Mahwah, New Jersey 07430

www.paulistpress.com

Printed and bound in the
United States of America

Table of Contents

For my students

Acknowledgments

For some time, I have had in mind writing a short uncomplicated book on Catholic parish administration. So many seminary students today have little to no experience in any kind of administration. Those that come from other countries are unfamiliar for the most part with the way parishes work in the United States. All of the students are usually pretty anxious about administration. They are good men, ready to preach and listen and minister the sacraments with confidence. But administration and what it entails is another matter. Thus this text.

I have been encouraged to write this by a number of people. I am indebted to Professor Charles Zech of the Church Management Institute at Villanova, who told me there is a need for this kind of book with an emphasis on relationships. My colleague, Professor Owen Cummings, has been a constant support and was not shy in telling me to "get it done!" I am thankful for that support and encouragement. I owe a special debt of gratitude to Monsignor Chuck Lienert, who for many years has been a mentor to me and taught me that "pastoring is about building relationships." My friend and colleague Reverend Rory Pitstick was a great help in preparing the final written version of the text. He has my thanks and gratitude.

For much of what is written here I am indebted to the years I spent in the Pastoral Center of the Archdiocese of Portland, Oregon, as an executive staff member. During those years I was virtually tutored by the staff of the Business Affairs Office, the Financial Services Office, and the Personnel Office: Paulette Furness, Delia Wilson, Rhonda Kwei, David Hodgin, Ken Scott, Leonard Vulsteke, Sandy Richards, Barbara Baltz, and Kate Belt. These committed, hard-working people and others taught me so much that I must say that much of what you read here is certainly what I picked up from working day-in day-out with them. I acknowledge them and thank them!

Finally, I would never have held the various executive positions I did were it not for my archbishops who placed their trust in me. I am grateful to then-Archbishop, now Cardinal William J. Levada, from whom I learned how to navigate through difficult situations with a sense of pastoral flexibility and respect. I am grateful to then-Archbishop, and now Cardinal Francis E. George, OMI, for teaching me how to do much listening before making a decision. And lastly, I am grateful to my present Archbishop, John G. Vlazny, for helping me to learn how to live with the hard, gray areas of administration.

Reverend Paul F. Peri, EdD
Mount Angel Seminary, St. Benedict, OR
January, 2010

Introduction

The well-publicized decline in the number of diocesan priests is bringing about a series of unintended consequences. One of these is that considerably less time is spent learning the skills and relational sensibilities of running a parish. In more and more dioceses, priests are being asked to become pastors after only one or two years as a parochial vicar. Unfortunately, what is being lost is the important time of "learning the ropes" (including the important administrative ropes) through being mentored by an older, more seasoned pastor. All of this is happening at a time when more attention is also being focused on the administrative demands of parishes. Where once dioceses and civil agencies made few administrative demands on the pastor of a parish—each parish was mostly administratively self-contained—now those demands in the forms of expectations of accuracy, transparency, and accountability in the various areas of business, finance, personnel, property, and insurance are the norm.

In larger parishes with a significant number of households, pastors are finding it necessary to hire laity to take over more of the administrative reins of a parish. Many of the laypeople hired have a background in the business world and in most instances willingly work for the parish at less than market-rate salaries. However, they have little to no background in parish or diocesan life beyond partic-ipation in the sacramental and perhaps the social life of their parishes and dioceses. What is missing in their expe-rience is a way of understanding how the parish and the diocese work and relate, and what pastoring means and how they are in fact involved in it.

Recently, I flew on a small, regional airline from an ordination of one of my students in Spokane in eastern Washington State back to Portland in western Oregon. I was fascinated to watch how the diverse landscapes flowed together, from the vast farmlands of eastern Washington and Oregon across the Cascade Mountains past Mount Hood, down the Columbia River into the green of western Oregon. From twenty thousand feet it is easy to grasp the lay of that landscape in a singular way. One can see how land, mountains, and river fit together to be the unique geographic piece of the country it is.

The purpose of this book is not to teach accounting, personnel management, or any of the other areas that com-prise parish administration. I intend to "fly at twenty thou-sand feet" over parish administration, if you will, to lay out in a broad, nontechnical overview what parish administration looks like and what makes it important. I want to show the person with little to no background in parish administration how the various pieces fit together in a pattern that makes parish administration unique. I want to show why adminis-tration of the parish is itself ministry. Lastly, I also want to point out some of the problem areas that need to be avoided.

This is a book especially for seminarians, but laypeople

starting out in parish ministry and the newly ordained will find it helpful as well. It is based on a course I teach at Mount Angel Seminary in Oregon. The course itself derives from some thirty-eight years as a priest and pastor as well as having served as clergy personnel director, vicar general, moderator of the curia, and vicar for finance in the Archdiocese of Portland in Oregon. It is my hope that it will help fill-in some of those mentoring gaps and allow seminarians and others with little parish experience to feel more confident in the ministry of administration in the parish.

CHAPTER ONE

Parish Administration in Context

A. The "Local Church"

It has always been interesting to me that wherever we go throughout the world, we are in some diocese or archdiocese of the Catholic Church. Canon Law refers to the diocese as a "particular church" or "a portion of the people of God entrusted to a Bishop."[1] In fact, the Universal Church is a communion of particular churches in union with one another and with the bishop of Rome, the pope. So, too, each particular church or diocese is also a communion of parish communities in union with one another and their bishop. These constitutive relationships are, in fact, acknowledged in the Eucharistic Prayer each time we celebrate Mass.

Here, then, is the foundational set of ecclesial relationships that form the broad context for the administration of the diocese and the parish. Bishops oversee their particular churches as pastors. They are assisted in this by priests whom the bishop sends to be pastors in the individual parishes of the diocese. The Rite of Ordination of a

Priest calls priests "coworkers" with the bishops.[2] So what the bishop does for the diocese as pastor and overseer, the priest as "coworker" is to do for his parish.

It is the primary duty of the bishop to keep the *koinonia*, or communion, within his own diocese amongst the various communities. Similarly, it is the chief task of the pastor of the parish to keep and strengthen the relationship between himself and his people, among the people themselves, and with their bishop. This relationship of *koinonia* is a defining characteristic that must mark the parish if it is to be Catholic in every sense and effective as the presence of Christ.

The bishop of a diocese is an overseer, and that includes administrative oversight. He sends priests to be pastors of the various parish communities with all that it entails administratively, but the bishop still has the ultimate responsibility for the well-running of the parishes and their compliance with the various civil laws and diocesan norms.

To help the bishop in his role of oversight, ordinarily he has a staff of various vicars and laypeople in his office, sometimes called the *chancery office* or *pastoral center*. The average diocesan office in the U.S., for example, has around eighty staff members.[3] In many dioceses it is likely there will be laypersons who have responsibility for business affairs, finances, personnel, insurance matters, properties, and the like. It is important to remember that they help the bishop carry out his administrative tasks. These lay officials should be seen as a resource for pastors and parishes. Some dioceses, for example, have a policy that sends someone from the pastoral center to perform some kind of high-level review or even an audit when a new pastor is appointed. Sometimes there might be an auditor who reviews the financial reports of parishes and their schools on a rotating basis throughout the diocese. These reviews and other kinds of audits, for example, personnel or insurance, by the diocese can be helpful for pastors and their staffs. When parish and diocese work together and have a mutual respect for each other, the result can be a learning experience for both, and the local church is strengthened.

I tell my students regularly that they should feel free to contact the diocese and ask for advice, especially because most pastors do not have expertise in the many areas of administration. Again, the diocesan office should be seen as a resource and should act as a resource for parishes. When in doubt, I tell the students, ask for help! Use common sense, yes, but unfortunately that is not always the case, and it can lead to some difficult consequences. How many contracts are entered into by a parish for equipment or services only to have the fine print become bad news! The diocesan officials can and will help, but they need to be asked before the steps are taken in the parish. I remember when I needed to replace a furnace in my parish church. Given the amount of money involved, I thought it would be wise for me to talk to the archdiocesan business office and review the matter. Luckily for me and the parish, the office was able to advise me that the furnace company had been very difficult to work with in another parish.

With that information, I was able to make a more informed decision in the matter.

B. Parish Administration— What It Is, and What It Is Not

I usually ask my class at the first meeting how much time they think they will be spending doing administration. They usually respond that it won't take much time. That, of course, may be true in a small rural parish, but even then, it is more likely that there will be more than one parish for the priest to pastor. The answer to the question is hard to determine since there are so many variables involved. In any case, I would not hesitate to say that, at least in my experience, it takes much more time than expected. Many pastors have told me over and over that they spend about *half* of their time in the demands of administration.

Because administration is part of pastoring, no matter how you see it or how much time it takes, it is curious to me why so many seminarians and priests want to place it on the sideline. Often, there is a kind of dualism in thinking that one particular aspect constitutes the "important" life of the parish while another aspect is the "not-so-important." Parish administration is seen as the latter. I always tell the students that if they keep that way of thinking, they will shortchange part of their ministry and perhaps be more likely to make mistakes, especially when it comes to personnel matters, in the name of getting back to what is "important." That is poor administration, pure and simple.

It is true that, as *Presbyterorum Ordinis* points out, the primary duty of the priest is the proclamation of the Gospel and the celebration of the Eucharist and the other sacraments, but that is not to say that administration of a parish is of little value or a waste of time.[4] In 1 Corinthians 12:27–31, St. Paul tells us that administration is a charism. If we priests do not see administration as a ministry, we probably will always be dissatisfied with it. If, however, administration is accepted as part of our pastoral ministry, it can be a kind of stewardship and part of the overall ministry of being the pastor of a community. The resources of a parish are the people, the finances, and the property. Good pastoring involves care for all three.

In his book, *The Effective Pastor: A Guide to Successful Ministry*, Louis W. Bloede describes administration as an "expression of ministry.…[involving] people.…a way of getting things done, a way of making things happen, a way of moving from point A to point B."[5] I like that way of describing administration because it is another way of describing *leadership*. Parish administration is not "nitpicking," "paper pushing," and all the other negative terms that are used by some to describe it. What it is, is *leaderership*, that is, building and sustaining relationships, and overseeing resources to bring about the parish's goals, which are nothing short of the mission of the Church.

C. The Pastor as Leader

In *Pastores Dabo Vobis*, Pope John Paul II, addressing the formation of future pastors, wrote: "Of special importance is the capacity to relate to others. This is fundamental for a person who is called to be responsible for a community.…"[6] These few lines are significant for all church workers, but especially for priests who would be pastors. Whatever else it is about, church work is about building and sustaining relationships! Whether those relationships are spiritual or administrative or personal, it is all about relationships!

Not too long ago, a national Catholic periodical carried an article by an anonymous parishioner who experienced a change in pastors. "The pastor," the writer said, "enjoys all power without the intuition or skill of leadership."[7] The upshot of this "'my way or the highway' approach to pastoral ministry resulted in 100% turnover in staff and three [permanent] deacons requesting transfers."[8]

To be sure, certainly not every new pastor causes division on first coming to his parish. One instance, however, is one too many. What often happens in these cases is parishioners leave the parish, some skip Sunday Mass, children are not baptized, and confirmations are delayed, because the parish is in disarray.

It is my experience that when the bishop sends a priest to be the pastor of a parish, he knows he is not sending the perfect man or a saint. The bishop, however, expects, and rightly so, that the one being sent is *mature*. By "mature," I mean that the man can develop a caring bond with his people and that the parish is not all about him. With help and even coaching, a mature priest can pastor a parish because he can *lead*.

About leadership, I would say this: Parish leadership is a charism, a gift for some, but also a skill that can be learned and developed, if one has a level of maturity. You cannot be an effective pastor unless you can lead. In a word, leadership in the parish means bringing out the grace of baptism in the baptized. The popular word is to *empower*. But the pastor as the leader, to my mind, does not so much empower—the Holy Spirit does that—as he prepares, helps, and defines for the community. In this, he affects the direction of the parish. These tasks cannot happen unless a pastor can work with all kinds of people in the parish.

When a priest comes to his new parish as a pastor or parochial vicar, people instinctively look to see whether this man can relate to others and thus lead them. It is important for a new priest to demonstrate by his behavior that he can and wants to make an emotional connection with the parish as well as provide for them spiritually. Indeed, if a pastor simply offers his people "services" without openness and a willingness to be part of their lives, the chances increase that the people will seek out some other parish or priest for counsel, serious confession, RCIA, weddings, and funerals.

Nowhere does the love for the people show itself more, I believe, than in the care for the sick and the dying and in the sacrament of reconciliation. I admonish my students that they will never go wrong if they pay special attention to the sick, the homebound, and the dying. It not only gives great comfort to the individual parishioner, but it comforts and strengthens the faith of others when the pastor spends time with these special parishioners. I have never seen a parish where the people did not learn quickly that the pastor is willing to go out of his way to visit the sick and spend time with the dying and their family members. The contrary is also true. If there is only perfunctory care for the sick and those who are dying, people have difficulty understanding why that is the case.

The same is also true with the sacrament of reconciliation. What people want to know is that the priest will listen and will assure them that God forgives. People come to the sacrament because they know they have fallen short and have sinned. What they need is assurance of grace and compassion. Leadership in this case does not mean telling people how to decide every aspect of their lives. Yes, people have a right to know what the Church teaches in the moral realm, absolutely, but spiritual leadership does not mean trying to take responsibility for the penitent's behavior.

I mentioned above the importance of making an emotional connection with the members of the parish in order to be effective. That is not to say there are no boundaries. Boundaries protect the people we serve since, by its very nature, the power in the pastoral relationship is not equal. Parish clergy and staff need to relate to those they serve, honoring them as persons. Appropriate boundaries serve that end. As one of my colleagues, Father Ray Carey, often says, it all comes down to having respect for people. If you observe

Jesus' behavior with people in the Gospels, it is always marked by Jesus' respect for each individual as a person.

Years ago, when I worked in our archdiocesan pastoral office, the then-executive director of the Oregon Catholic Conference, Mr. Bob Castagna, once described for me what he called the "Law of the Three D's." He said these three words were always a reminder to him in his position to act responsibly and respectfully. They are a good and constant reminder of appropriate boundaries: "Discretion, Diplomacy, and Decorum." I emphasize these three essentials with students because, like Bob, I believe they are reminders that need to be part of one's thinking in pastoral ministry as we interact with people. *Discretion* means the pastor needs to have prudential judgment in his actions and words. *Diplomacy* means the pastor needs to have tact. He can negotiate where there are various opinions involved. Finally, *decorum* dictates what is appropriate behavior and conforms to clerical and ethical standards.

D. Parish Policy and Decision Making

If anything defines what I would describe as absolutely essential to setting policies and making decisions in the parish community, I would say it is *collaboration*. Indeed, a successful pastoral leader today would do well to view collaboration as a way of administering all aspects of parish life. Marti Jewell and David Ramey have remarked that collaboration in the areas of "professional practice, empowerment of the gifts of others, and the use of prayer and prayerful discernment with parishioners"[9] is a sign that the parish is vibrant and alive. Parishioners support decisions and policies at every level that are seen as flowing from an approach to the parish that is respectful of each baptized member's gifts.

To be sure, the pastor is *the* leader. It is he that the bishop sends to care for the parish and lead it. Having said that, it should be apparent that the pastor or other leaders, but especially the pastor, cannot give care or lead—including implementing administrative and pastoral policies—unless he knows the people. In order to understand the people and their points of view, he needs to consult. The pastor is the leader, but he is not the parish! Leadership demands consultation and being able to work well with others.

I recall a parish in which the new pastor followed a well-loved and collaborative pastor. Unwisely, the new pastor came into the church before his first Sunday and, without talking to anyone, simply changed the seating arrangement and the placement of the musicians. People were rightly upset with the situation. It came across as a kind of power play, as if to say "I am the pastor! I am in charge! It will go my way!" True or not, it seemed that way to lots of parishioners, and they wanted no part in that kind of community.

E. Pastoral and Finance/ Administrative Councils

Happily, the Church has provided an excellent forum in which to seek out the views of the faithful about the direction in which the parish ought to go to achieve its mission, and that is the *pastoral council*. The purpose of pastoral councils is precisely to do pastoral planning—going from A to B!

It is important to distinguish between what are called *parish councils* and the *pastoral council*. When I was a young priest, the parish council model was common. The overall idea was that every group and organization would be represented at a meeting with the pastor. The task of these representatives was to give information to the pastor and the other members. Needless to say, it was pretty routine. The joke was "Why do I have to go to a meeting after work on a weekday night to help the altar guild decide whether they should have ham or turkey at their dinner?" Because these meetings were simply a matter of sharing data, people lost interest and the model failed, though unfortunately, many parishes still use this model.

In distinction, the pastoral council model is one of doing pastoral planning for the parish, which is more than a matter of information. In this, pastoral planning answers some basic questions: Who makes up our parish demographically? Who are we as a Catholic parish? What is our mission? What are the spiritual and corporal works that are demanded of us as Catholic Christians in this particular context? How do we worship? How do we hand on the faith to the next generation of parishioners? How do we evangelize? How do we interact with non-Catholics and the wider community? And, of course, what are the resources of the parish community to fulfill our plan?

I believe that pastoral planning, in whatever precise form it is undertaken, should always involve several elements: (a) prayer, (b) study and reflection on the mission and ministries of the parish, (c) the review and evaluation of the current activities of the parish, (d) a study of the needs that are not being met, and (e) the study of the resources of the parish, including the faithful (who are the most important resource of a parish!), the finances, and the property.[10]

Finally, the planning process culminates in a written document with some provision for how goals and objectives will be implemented and eventually evaluated. Naturally, this document in its final form must be approved by the pastor. However, it should be recognized that what is truly important is not the written document so much as that the parish membership all know where the parish is going and how it will get there. In presenting and explaining this, the pastor will be the leader.

Church law mandates that each parish have a finance or administrative council.[11] This council is consultative to the pastor. But here again, the wise, collaborative pastor seeks advice and a consensus around the policies having to do with the material and financial administration of the parish in line with diocesan norms. These resources are not the pastor's personal possessions. He is a steward for the community. The resources are to be used in support of the parish mission, which the pastoral council has described for the community.

Depending on the size of the parish, it might be wise for the pastor to find and appoint parishioners with specific skills and knowledge for council membership. I can think of many times when it would have been helpful to have had someone in personnel management to consult on the council. When we think of the makeup of a finance council, we obviously think of people with an accounting or banking background. That, of course, makes sense. But I would encourage pastors to consider small business owners, as well as teachers and others who might have a broader perspective on matters that come before the council. I always wanted someone on the council who was committed to stewardship and could make the case for it, rather than assuming that traditional fundraising based on the budget was the way to go.

A thread has run through this chapter, and that is the centrality of relationships. The context for being a pastor (and I do not believe this is an overstatement) is his own relationship to the Risen Lord, to his bishop, to his presbyterate, and especially his people in the parish. It is no easy task and takes skill and knowledge to be able to build and sustain those relationships, but that is exactly what the parish priest is called to do. In being this kind of pastor and leader, the priest is supported by the councils of the parish, by his staff, and always, by all the volunteers and others who join in making the parish the Body of Christ in the world.

Having described the broad context for leading the parish, I now turn to the area that I call "general business." In this chapter, I want to raise a few matters pertaining to parish and diocesan legal structure as well as the practical working structure of a parish. Also, we will discuss good business practice for the parish.

Questions for Discussion

1. How do you understand parish administration? What is its role in parish life? What makes parish administration a ministry?
2. Who makes the day-to-day financial decisions in your diocese or religious province or community?
3. Does your diocese have an administrative manual? Is there an employee handbook?
4. What would you describe as some examples of excellent leadership from a pastor?
5. What is the difference between the "parish" council and a "pastoral" council?

CHAPTER TWO
General Business

A. The Big Picture

When many professional people begin a new job, they are given a position description, shown their office, introduced to colleagues, and then they start to work. In places that offer a bit more of an introduction to the organization, the new employee is given a view of the entire structure, informed as to how operations proceed at each level, and told which protocols are used at which levels. This is obviously helpful information for doing one's job well.

While parishes are not businesses in themselves, it is important to recognize that they do parallel small businesses in some respects. For instance, it would be wise for the first-time pastor or the new employee to review the legal structure in which they are working. Many dioceses are legally a *corporation sole*. That means that the diocese, for civil (as distinct from canonical and ecclesial) purposes, is a legal entity of a sole incorporated office, occupied by a sole individual, ordinarily the diocesan bishop. The benefit of the corporation sole is that it allows the corporation to pass vertically from one office holder to his successor. This gives legal continuity with each subsequent office holder. So, when a diocesan bishop is moved or dies or retires, the next bishop can pick up the office and an orderly transfer of property takes place.[1]

At the same time, many parishes are incorporated as a *religious corporation*. This kind of corporation is a religious nonprofit organization, incorporated usually by a state, and operates under the regulations of the governmental official holder of records. Ordinarily, if parishes are incorporated in this fashion, the pastor and some parishioners, as well as a diocesan official, sit on the corporation board. Each state has its own way of constituting these corporations, which is why it is necessary to understand the exact way one's own state laws approach the matter. Your diocesan officials should be able to explain how the laws apply to your parish.[2]

It is important to understand these two notions of corporations. Among other things, organizations set up in these ways have their own obligations, such as an *annual meeting*. An understanding of these legal concepts will influence the practical decisions that pastors have to make on a regular basis. For example, if I am the pastor of a parish that has a building project, or if someone offers to give my parish real property, or if I have to purchase a copy machine for the parish office, what is the extent of my authority to sign documents? In other words, what is the extent of my authority, given the fact that I operate in a corporate structure or even two? What demands come from the diocesan corporation, and what demands are present at the parish corporate level? Each diocese will have its own policies and protocols with respect to these kinds of corporate matters.

Perhaps nowhere is corporate involvement more delicate than in the area of personnel. When, for example, the diocese devises a handbook for use throughout the parishes and schools, the pastor and other staff members need to be aware of all the policies in the handbook, because they are not only operating on behalf of their parish, but they are also acting as agents of the diocesan corporation.

The fact is, we live in a litigious age. Gone are the days when people would not think of suing their parish or the diocese if they believe they have been treated unfairly. Few employees will simply walk away from a disagreement because the parish or diocese is a party in the disagreement.

B. The Practical Working Structure

It can be overwhelming to be pastor of a large urban or suburban parish for the first time. It is reassuring to the new pastor to know that he has all the parish staff and school staff he needs to minister to the people. In some parishes, the number of parish and school staff can be thirty or more! It may well be a task for the pastor to collaborate with so many staff members, but he needs to find real ways that will allow the entire staff to describe their vision of being a parish community. The most common way is to have staff meetings on a regular basis for the purpose of sharing information and building a bond as a staff. To be sure, having a large staff calls for a sense of organization and accountability. It is important that every employee knows who reports directly to whom. In these situations, good administration involves the recognition that the pastor can and should delegate, but he can never abdicate his responsibility. The bottom line is the pastor is responsible for the well running of the administration of the parish. My general rule of thumb is: hire the most capable people you can afford for the job and then let them do it! Tell them what the job is (position description) and how you expect them to act in carrying out the assigned work—professionally. This includes being able to know when they need to confer with you as pastor about a decision, and when they don't.

I remember one situation in which a pastor was sent to a parish with a school. Since he disliked administration and did not want to be involved with it, especially in the school, he turned it all over to the parish business manager, including the school. As a result, the business manager was the de facto "superintendent" of the school, and there was a great deal of confusion among staff and parents about who was really in charge. It doesn't take a great deal of imagination to recognize that this is a set-up for problems and a lack of morale among employees—"He doesn't really like those of us who work in the school!"

New pastors are often counseled by other pastors "not to change anything for one year." This is sage advice, a way of saying: Learn the practical working structure you are in first! I tell my students to spend some time *observing* when they arrive as the new parochial vicar or pastor. Making even some small decisions too soon can be problematic. I remember a priest who became the pastor of a rural parish that still had the custom of ringing bells during the elevation in the Eucharistic Prayer. The sound drove him crazy, and he did away with those bells in very short order. It most likely would have been a minor matter had he explained his rationale to the people. But when the bells were just gone, he got a reaction he did not expect and did not like. The practical working order of the liturgy had been changed by the pastor without acknowledging its importance for a large number of worshipers.

Always take note of the various preexisting relationships in the parish. Who reports to whom *unofficially*? Which groups in the parish volunteer the most time and talent? Who has been in the parish office the longest? What are the strengths and weaknesses of the individual staff members and council members? Which parishioners come forward immediately upon your arrival with tasks that they would like you to take on or changes that you should make? Get the lay of the land; and frankly, learn where the various "seats of power" reside. Doing this will help avoid any "minefields" that are out there and that every organization has.

C. Advisability of Consultation

When a pastor or parish worker is operating with either the wrong information or lack of information, critical situations can easily go from bad to worse. Employment is one of those areas. I remember a situation in which a person who had been hired at the parish level was not told about medical and retirement benefits. The upshot was the employee went to the hospital emergency room and said she worked for the parish and had insurance—only to be informed that she was not on the diocesan plan! Someone at the parish didn't realize that it was a *parish* obligation to register parish employees on the diocesan insurance plan.

In another case, a pastor did not enroll a new employee for retirement benefits. The employee was merely told there were benefits and it was left at that. Several years later, a diocesan review found that the employee had never been registered for the retirement plan. The parish and the diocese had to enter into an agreement to bring the employee up to speed. It wasn't inexpensive.

It is wise not only to be acquainted with all applicable laws—whether regarding employment or other especially serious matters—but also to readily admit what one does not know or understand and ask for help. One can never go wrong if one simply calls a diocesan official to review the issues and decisions at hand.

Questions for Discussion

1. What kind of corporate structure is your diocese or religious community? Are parishes separately incorporated?

2. In the largest parishes in your diocese, how many staff members would be the norm? With a school?

3. Does your diocese provide a sample "position description" for the various parish positions, for example, director of religious education, office manager, pastoral associate?
4. What is your experience of "seats of power" in the parish?
5. What are the things that you would want to make sure you do in terms of relationships with staff and people on first becoming a pastor?

CHAPTER THREE
Personnel

A. The Many Hats of the Pastor

I mentioned in chapter 2 that the whole area of personnel could be sensitive for the pastor as parish administrator. While it is true that human resources is governed by parish and diocesan policies and civil laws, it is also true for pastors that it is an area of special care and concern. Pastors want to get along with employees not only because they are employees, but because many employees are also parishioners. So pastors wear both administrative and pastoral hats, among others. Problems can result when the hats get mixed up and either the pastor or the employee doesn't know which hat the pastor is wearing.

Priests want to take pastoral care of parishioners. That is the hat of "parish priest." It is the hat most folks look to the priest for as well. But the pastor also wears some other hats, for example, those of employer, administrator, colleague, even friend. When I talk to my students about this, they usually see little to no likelihood of these relationships interfering with one another. The students are taken aback when I tell them that whenever I began pastoral work at a new parish, I always informed my staff that I could not hear their confessions or give serious personal counsel. Someone always immediately asks, "But what if you are in a rural parish in the panhandle of Idaho and your business manager or the director of religious education comes and asks to go to confession? Would you turn him or her away?" It's not an easy answer, but I insist that *yes*, I would turn that person away! I would have to, and here's why: Let us say that you are the pastor of a parish with a bookkeeper. Let us say further that the bookkeeper asks to go to confession, and you agree. Now let's say that the bookkeeper confesses that she or he has been secretly taking funds from the parish for some years and it amounts to more than five thousand dollars! Now what? Or what if the DRE confesses that she has had an affair with the permanent deacon? Again, now what? There is nothing you can really do with that kind of knowledge, and I would guess that it will color the way you look at the people involved and how you relate to them.

In sum, we always need to be aware of which hat we are wearing as a church worker, especially pastors and parochial vicars. Being leaders in the parish community, we are always coming into contact with people in different ways, from giving pastoral care to socializing, and it is healthy for one's self and the people if we understand where the boundaries of those relationships are.

B. Some Mistakes to Avoid in Personnel Decisions

From my experience, here are a few areas of special consideration.

Types of Employees

Make sure you know the differences between *exempt* and *nonexempt* employees and *independent contractors*. What are "exempt employees" exempt from? They are exempt from the Fair Labor Standards Act of 1938.[1] These are the people on your staff that are paid to "do a job" (the director of religious education, for example), as distinct from those paid "by the hour" (such as the parish secretary) and who are entitled to overtime pay. Usually those who are exempt are those who supervise two or more people and have the authority to hire, fire, discipline, and make salary increase recommendations, or the position they fill requires a special course of study, such as a college degree.

According to the above definition, most pastors and parochial vicars would qualify as exempt as well. Also exempt are teachers, principals, business managers, and other qualified professional lay ministers. Maintenance employees, bookkeepers, and janitorial staff are examples of nonexempt employees.

Perhaps it is not the case as much today as we become more sophisticated in parish administration, but in the past, people were listed as "independent contractors" when they really weren't. Musicians are the prime example. They were seen as contracted service providers because they came in for weekend Masses and were not perceived as being "on staff." However, the law has a long list of reference points to determine who qualifies as an independent contractor, and most parish musicians would not satisfy all of the legal criteria to be considered as providing "contracted services." Keep in mind that when speaking of contracted services, in general, we are speaking about people such as landscaping workers, who have all their own materials, set their own schedules, and do their jobs with little or no direction. They really are "independent."

Timesheets

Every employee ought to fill out a timesheet. Non-exempt employees will obviously be keeping track of their hours for payment, especially since they are paid overtime. Exempt employees will keep track of their time off. There is a tendency to avoid tracking time away for exempt people, whether for sick leave or vacation, because it seems like "just more paper work" for someone who is not an hourly worker. However, exempt employees may at some point leave the employ of a parish or be fired, and the parish administration will have to determine the amount of vacation time these employees have accrued. How do you fairly compensate someone for accrued vacation time when no one has an accurate record of the amount of time that was or wasn't used? In such cases, the parish can only accept the word of the exiting employee.

Reference Checks on Employees

Most dioceses have some basic steps for new hires, including requiring a signed application with a place for listing prior employment with the dates of that employment. One of the most difficult things to convince some pastors to do is a thorough reference check, accounting for gaps in employment. To be sure, it can be tedious making numerous phone calls, but this kind of diligence is always worth the effort. When it isn't done, there will usually be problems. I can recall a case in which the pastor did not do sufficient background checking and ended up hiring someone who had a record of a financial crime against a church in another state. The job the person was hired for was bookkeeper! When the new pastor came, he began to realize that something was not quite right with the financial records, and the whole situation came to light.

It seems so obvious, but it bears repeating: references need to be carefully checked! In doing the reference check, I always recommend that the hiring person be sure to talk to the prospective new hire's *supervisor*. It has been known to happen that people who had a problem with their last supervisor will put down the name of a friend as a contact person at the former job. Always ask: Were you this person's supervisor? While the prior supervisor's evaluation may not be the deciding factor in hiring, it needs to be part of the discussion for a complete picture of past performance. Also, it is good to ask if there is any other person at the former place of employment that you should talk to. Another good question to ask when doing the background check is whether the former employer would hire the person in question again?

After verifying a prospective employee's professional competence, my next major concern would be whether the person can get along with others. As I have said, parish work is all about relationships. That is why finding out how the perspective hire worked with others is so important. Being able to work as a team member and get along with people in the parish who can sometimes be unhappy about something is essential. I have found over the years that there are some people who just do not know how to work as team members. Perhaps they were self-employed most of their adult lives, or perhaps they have simply never worked as part of a team. Working with others is a skill in itself, and a crucial one.

Employee Termination

At some point, all parish administrators will have to deal with this situation. There are two points to keep in mind. First, termination must be based on objective behavioral data. If the employee cannot get along with other staff or parishioners, or cannot or will not fulfill the job requirements, or if there are other serious issues, it is *imperative* that you as supervisor have documented the offending behaviors. When you call the diocesan human resources office to report terminating an employee, the first thing they will ask is: What documentation do you have? If you have none, you will be asked to start compiling it, and that will lengthen the remedy process.

Second, I would say that termination should never come as a surprise to the employee involved. Part of the documentation should include conversations that you as supervisor have had with the employee about fixing whatever the problem is. Here again, it is about a relationship, and there is a need to be objective, clear, and fair. The record should show that, when all is said and done. One more suggestion: When it comes to the final meeting with the employee, always have a third party in the room. The person is not there to do anything but be a certain non-emotional presence. That is helpful because letting someone go is always an emotional point for everyone involved, even when it seems to be accepted well by the employee.

A Few Other Pitfalls to Avoid

Never tell an employee that he or she is permanent. In one case a pastor, with all the best motives in the world, told an employee that she would always have her job in the parish. But when a new pastor came, he wanted to make some changes that included letting the "permanent" employee go. As one can imagine, the matter was not resolved without hurt feelings on all sides.

Be aware of the need for a *compensation system* to determine salary. Without some kind of scale, someone who answers the phone in the parish office might keep getting yearly increases that eventually result in the person making a salary that is far out of proportion to their work responsibilities. Pay what the position is worth! A salary scale, whether one from the diocese or one devised by the parish finance council, will support the fair compensation of all the parish employees.

C. Matters That Need Attention

Some pastors have a tendency to avoid performance issues. It is helpful to review employee performance on some kind of regular basis. I have found that it is supportive and helpful to meet with new hires a month after they begin working, then again in two or three more months. By that time, they are getting a good feel for the job and have the opportunity— they don't have to *request* it—for asking their procedural and other questions. Once the employee is fully on board, the yearly review will suffice, provided there are no issues that demand immediate attention.

We may not think of a performance review as being supportive, but it certainly can be, even when some behavior needs correction. I have found that most employees like to know where they stand. They are trying to do a good job. If we review their job description with them and ask how they are attending to the various points, it gives them a chance to describe their successes. It is also the time for you, as supervisor, to thank them for their good work and presence in the parish.

I would strongly suggest that pastors, especially new pastors who have been in their position for a year or so, discuss with their parish advisors a performance review for *themselves*. I understand that the thought of such a thing can be threatening, but it doesn't have to be. There are any number of ways of approaching this kind of evaluation, but of course, the real question is: What do I as pastor want to know about my leadership in the various areas that comprise parish life? The straightforward questions I like to ask myself as a pastor are: What do I do well? Where do I need to improve? I find that if I am willing to look at myself objectively as a pastor, people respect that, especially the councils and staff. Remember, this is not about my popularity as pastor, it is about my effectiveness as pastor. Without helpful, objective information, it is hard to assess. Besides, my experience is that one gets more support and thanks than anything else!

Next, I would like to say a word about volunteers. As every pastor knows, they are the backbone of the parish. Without them we would have a very difficult time meeting all the demands of parish life. It is important for pastors and others to see these volunteers as parish ministers. These are people who are putting into practice their baptismal call to serve. So, really, they are more than volunteers. They are true ministers in the parish by virtue of their baptismal anointing. My point here is we need to recognize and encourage that kind of presence in the parish in important ways. Yes, of course, we need to thank them publicly, but we also need to thank them personally. Once as a pastor, I went to a candy maker at Christmas time and asked him to make a special little box of chocolates for each volunteer in the parish. Because I ordered so many, I got a good price. I put a note on each box and thanked the person individually for what he or she did. I have never had such a huge response. More than one person said that she had never been thanked. I doubt that was the case, but because volunteers are with us so much around the office and the church, we can easily overlook them. I was glad this time I was able to say *thank you*! I would also add that we should make sure that all the lay ministers have whatever kind of education or skills development that will help them do the work they are being asked to volunteer for.

When I talk to pastors about teaching parish administration in the seminary, inevitably they ask me to remind the future parochial vicars that, while they are ordained to the priesthood, they are not independent workers in the parish. In short, the parochial vicar works for the pastor. I hear reports now and then from pastors saying that their parochial vicars sometimes change various procedures and liturgical practices on the spot. This can cause confusion among liturgical ministers and among office staff. My point here is certainly not to shake a finger at new priests and their energy, but to say that the relationship between the pastor and his assistant sets a certain tone in the parish. If they are not on the same page, then inevitably tensions arise. Unchecked, these tensions become obvious to the parishioners, and the parish can divide. My suggestion to both pastors and their vicars is to talk about procedural matters, especially the liturgy, before a difference arises.

In sum, all of this leads to saying that a good, healthy parish workplace ought to be marked by clear expectations, a sense of responsibility, quality communication, the presence of boundaries, and accountability. These provide for healthy and effective relations among staff. Remember: In the long run, it is all about the mission of the parish. How effective that mission is depends to a large extent on the working relationships of pastors, parish staffs, and volunteers.

Questions for Discussion

1. Name the "hats" that you think most pastors wear. How can those hats complement one another? Where do you think conflicts might occur?

2. Have you ever been an "hourly" or nonexempt employee? What was your job? Have you been an exempt employee? What position did you have? In either case, what did you look for in a good supervisor? How might those characteristics apply to you as a pastor?

3. Does your diocese have a salary scale for lay employees? What benefits, for example, health insurance, are offered?

4. Have you ever hired someone for a position? Describe the process you used to fill the position.

5. How would you conduct a yearly performance review with an employee? What if the review were specifically about poor performance, for example, consistent tardiness?

CHAPTER FOUR
Finances

One morning I opened my e-mail and found a letter from a friend of mine who is pastor of a suburban parish in his archdiocese. I have known him for years, and he is a terrific pastor in every way. That is why I was surprised when he wrote that he had just found out that his church had been robbed of the Sunday collection for the second time in two weeks!

Apparently, there was a gap between the drop door and the sacristy safe into which the collections were deposited. The thief was able to insert a device, possibly a coat hanger, and fish out the collection bags. There were no signs of forced entry, and to this day the parish is not sure who did it or exactly how it happened. Needless to say, locks were changed, motion detectors were added, and a new safe purchased as well. For the pastor, those changes were the easy part. What was more difficult and downright embarrassing was telling the parishioners!

I raise this because, while it certainly is not an everyday occurrence, it does happen that parish funds get compromised. So, I would advise anyone who is becoming a new pastor to start by being *observant*. Because you are coming into a new situation, you have a perspective that is fresh and you are in a position to initiate discussion with staff and councils about areas that should be reviewed for safety of funds. The first six months of an assignment should probably be full of all kinds of questions about parish life and practice. People expect it!

A. Possible Problem Areas

Some security issues come to mind right away. Every parish has its own procedures for handling money, but it is precisely those procedures that should be reviewed with advisors periodically to ensure the safety of the funds, as well as the good name and reputation of all the people who handle the funds.

In this regard, there are two areas that deserve special attention. One is what happens to the collection from the time it is placed in one basket in the sanctuary (which is quite common, almost universal now in parishes) until the time it is counted. The next area that deserves special attention is when, where, who, and how many people count the collection. A basic security concept is *dual custody*: the monies should never be in the sole possession of any one person during the time they are taken up, counted, and deposited.

The use of tamper-proof bags provided by a bank has proven to be of great help in securing the collection. When I receive the collection at the Presentation of the Gifts at Mass, it is placed in front of the altar until immediately after Mass, when two designated people take it to the sacristy to be immediately and quickly placed in the tamper-proof bags and sealed. Then both people sign the numbered bag, and it is placed in a secure drop-safe. Obviously, there can be some variations on this method, depending on the particular circumstances of the parish. The main point is that the collection is always in the presence of at least two people until it is literally dropped in the holding safe until counted.

A word here about those old safes that are used in parishes: Most of them have been in the parish for a long time, and no one really knows how many people over the years have been given the combination. I would advise having the combination changed when you come in as a new pastor. I would tell my finance council and staff that I am changing the combination, but importantly, I would also say that anyone who believes that he or she should have the combination should come and see me. People can get hurt feelings when they have had "special access" and then the situation changes. The same could be said about keys to various doors.

When the counting team signs in to count the collection, there are always at least two people, and preferably three, and they are not husband-and-wife teams. The counting itself takes place in a locked, out-of-the-way room. At one parish where I was pastor, the collection was counted on a card table in the open front parlor as people came and went. I asked if we couldn't do the counting in a more appropriate place. Remember, the point of all this is to ensure the financial integrity of the parish and your administration as the pastor.

Another area that could be problematic is that of bank statements. In this computer age of online banking, there may be parishes that choose not to receive their canceled checks with a copy of the bank statement, but I would not be among them. I had the practice of having the unopened bank statement put on my desk when it came. I would then go through the canceled checks, and if I had any questions about what a certain check was for, I could ask. I took this as an oversight responsibility as the administrator of the parish. The staff knew it and accepted it as such. Indeed, more than once, it led to a good conversation about our programs and the materials we used for them. Once I looked at the returned checks, they were given to the bookkeeper so that accounts could be reconciled.

It is important to keep track of check stock. I recall a case where someone took a numbered check from the bottom of the supply box and used it for fraudulent purposes. No one knew about it for a time because when checks were written, they came off the computer in perfect numerical order. Nothing was seemingly out of place. Advice: Keep check stock locked up!

As a pastor, you will spend more time than you would undoubtedly like being a signer on parish checks. I insist on two signatures on every check, and my signature is always the last one. Be sure to attach a "backup" to each check you're going to sign. Backup is a bill for services, a purchase order, or something that explains why the check was written. Tell staff that if they are going to ask for reimbursement for a lunch meeting or whatever it might be, they need to present the appropriate backup as well.

Never, ever sign a blank check for anyone, or worse yet, have a rubber or computer signature stamp made. This comes up when, for example, someone on staff is going to an outlet or big-box store for supplies such as paper, cleaners, coffee for meetings, etcetera. It is better to go along with the person making the purchases and fill out the check yourself. Or, you can ask the staff person to put it on his or her charge card and then get reimbursed. I would caution against allowing employees or volunteers to use parish credit cards. While they are certainly convenient, they are open for abuse. Indeed, a parish in which I have provided weekend coverage recently had a note from the pastor in the parish bulletin saying that the business manager was let go because of "inappropriate use of parish credit cards." It undoubtedly means more work, but I believe that a parish is better off in the long run without parish credit cards.

B. Finance Council

Pastors can get an untold amount of help from their finance or administrative council members. They are selected by the pastor precisely for their expertise in various areas of accounting and their business skills. Most finance council members are eager to be of service, whether working with the bookkeeper on the accounts or reviewing policies and procedures. It is really up to the pastor to train the council members on their advisory duties as a council. I would urge pastors to encourage council members to ask any questions they have and, particularly, not to be shy about questions of internal controls. If the pastor and the finance council are diligent and proactive, unpleasant financial scandals will not happen in their parish.

It is most appropriate for the pastor to place the finance council's work in a spiritual setting of service to the church and stewardship of the parish resources. Their presence and advice is a grace for the pastor and the parish, and should be understood and presented in that light. A yearly thank-you dinner or other celebration would not be out of place either.

C. The Budget

Canon Law requires that administrators keep accurate records of income and expenditures, as well as draw up an accounting of their administration each year. Administrators are, and I would guess most dioceses demand it, urged to have an annual budget of income and expenses.[1]

Some of my students, especially those from other countries, find the area of budgeting to be intimidating. Most have little to no background in money matters beyond keeping household accounts. I assure them that it might seem intimidating because of the language accountants and business people use, but as pastors, they do not have to be accountants. They should think of it as they do their own personal budgeting—money comes in and goes out! Think ahead about how much you will need for the various things you buy.

Let us say that a budget is an estimate of what the parish will take in as *income* and what it will spend as *expense*. A budget is made for a certain period of time, ordinarily for the fiscal year, which goes from July 1st until June 30th. Remember that a budget is simply a tool for parish management purposes, and it is organized around certain determined categories called the *chart of accounts*. These include *salaries, utilities, youth ministry, and liturgy,* among others. Obviously, having a budget cannot make the collection or other sources of income go up or down. The budget simply estimates based on the prior year what will come in to the parish as income and what the parish will need to spend to carry out its mission.

As a pastor, I found that by the end of March, I could have a pretty reliable estimate of what the ordinary income of the parish would be for that fiscal year. I also knew, from the expenses during that time, what I would most likely be needing to spend next year for so-called *hard costs*, that is, the cost of heat and lights, water, salaries and the diocesan tax on the collection (*cathedraticum*), and so forth. I hasten to add that it was the parish business manager that produced the information for my review. The computer makes gathering the data rather simple. Together we figured what increases would be likely, and where. From that, we prepared a draft of the next year's budget for the parish finance council's review and comment, and a final version was recommended to me as pastor. The whole process took several months' time and allowed, of course, for input from staff, pastoral council, and others regarding parish needs.

Always remember to put some monies aside in the budget as savings, even if it is a small or token amount. The day will come when something such as a furnace or the copy machine will give up altogether, and you will need to replace the equipment in a hurry. It is easier to ask the parishioners to contribute if "the parish" can make a cash commitment up front toward the project. Then, too, there was the year that we got hit with a huge ice storm on Christmas Eve and Christmas Day. All Masses had to be canceled. Needless to say, I was grateful that I had some savings to fall back on since the monthly bills come no matter how bad the weather is.

I recommend making a habit of asking your diocesan office to send out projected budget information that applies to all the parishes. My experience is that diocesan offices will give their best estimates of how health insurance, property insurance, and other costs are trending, so parish estimates can be as accurate as possible, given staff and insured property. The more good information you have, the more accurate and helpful will be the budget.

Pastors and finance councils should be clear, systematic, transparent, and regular in reporting to the parish on financial matters. Pastors and councils need to remind themselves that parish money is not *their* money. It belongs to the parish and they are simply stewards for the good of that community.

Making a statement about the financial state of the parish in the Sunday bulletin is not a bad idea, but such statements don't really tell the whole story about where parishioners' dollars are being spent. It is important to tell the community how the mission of the Church is being carried out by means of their giving. I used to put out "pastoral letters" to the parish, giving the people what I believe was good information. I might include the number of baptisms for a certain period of time. Or I might describe some of the people who came to our church door asking for help of various kinds. For example, we had a lunch for the homeless during the week, so I would remind parishioners how many people were being fed or how many boxes of food were given out from the parish pantry. In this way, parishioners were made aware of how the parish was caring for others, as Jesus taught us.

However one decides to get information out to the people—the parish web site is excellent—they have a right as members of the community to be kept informed. In addition, they get excited to know that there is a certain leaven in the parish. People want their parish to be vibrant and alive, and part of administration is to find practical ways not only to make that happen, but to let people know that it is happening. Call it the "ministry of encouragement." Again, it is about leadership and fostering relationships of the people among themselves!

Some dioceses have a system of internal audits or financial reviews. Before a pastor takes over a new parish and as the former pastor leaves, the auditor comes in and works with the pastor and the parish business manager or bookkeeper to see that accounts and records are in order, diocesan policies are being followed, and accounting questions are answered. In my archdiocese, the pastors are genuinely happy about the program. The auditors are professional, extremely helpful in answering questions, and the whole process is really one of continuing education for everyone involved. Pastors have told me that this is the kind of help from the diocesan office that they really appreciate, because from these meetings they gain more confidence in their administrative skills.

D. The Priest's Own Finances

While it is not directly related to the purpose of this chapter, it seems important to say a few words about a topic that is usually a mystery to my students, and that is the area of their own financial position. While diocesan clergy have no vow of poverty and can own property and inherit, they are by the very nature of their vocation to lead a life of evangelical simplicity. What that means in practice is ordinarily left up to the individual priest, but simplicity of lifestyle is important for the credibility of his witness as the pastor.

My concern here, however, is that most diocesan priests will need some personal savings for their retirement. I see retirement monies as a three-legged stool: One leg is Social Security, another is any diocesan retirement plan, and the third is the priest's own savings. Whether Social Security, as we now know it, will be viable in the future is beyond the scope of this discussion. Also, each diocese has its own approach to priests' retirement benefits. Some are quite generous and others are more modest.

A priest benefits not only himself, but also his diocese, if he is able to help defray the costs associated with nursing home care in his old age, or bring in special help where he lives to do various tasks of housekeeping and the like. All of this will take money, of course.

In order to have the amount of funds required for his portion of that three-legged stool, the priest needs to have savings. The way to accumulate those savings is to start early! I emphasize this with the seminarians in my class because they seem to have an unshakable belief or sense that they and their money matters will always be taken care of by their bishop or someone else. The reality is that the bishop expects his priests to live simply and do their part in preparation for retirement with whatever salary they receive.

I tell my students that when they are first assigned to a parish, they should ask about the instruments provided through the diocese for retirement savings. Starting early allows one to take advantage of the "miracle of compounding." Just a small amount invested wisely each month in some tax-deferred account will provide beneficial savings in the long run. Consider how a penny that doubles every day will grow to five million dollars in thirty days! Here again, we see the value of long-term compounding and the value of starting early.[2]

Besides starting early, it is important that the saver have a plan. When will one be able to retire, and how long will the savings need to last? Part of the investing plan should include answering the question of one's tolerance for risk. If one is risk-adverse, then riskier investments such as stocks might be a smaller percentage of one's investments. Bonds or more stable investments might make up a larger percentage.

In sum, start to save early on, have a plan, decide how much risk you can live with and, importantly, get some fully independent and objective advice from a professional so that an informed decision can be made. Never be afraid to ask questions about the professional's compensation. Here again, if you have doubts, ask the finance people in the diocesan office. I have never known them not to be of help to priests.

Questions for Discussion

1. What might be some appropriate questions about parish finances that you could discuss with the pastor or business manager when you are first appointed to a parish?
2. What is the difference between the work of the finance council and the work of the pastoral council? In what ways might they overlap?
3. In the parish budget, which are "fixed" or "hard" costs (for example, heating fuel) and which would be examples of so-called "soft" costs?
4. What is the age of retirement for priests in your diocese? What retirement benefits do you expect to receive from your diocese when you reach that age?
5. In today's dollars, how much money do you think you will need in retirement altogether in order to provide for yourself in old age? Of that amount, how much will come from a diocesan plan?

CHAPTER FIVE

Property

A. Sales, Acquisition, Alienation

Book 5, "The Temporal Goods of the Church," in the *Code of Canon Law*, contains over fifty separate canons dealing with the acquisition, administration, and alienation (disposal) of church goods. These canons describe not only the complex nature of the subject, but also the insistence that the use or disposal of goods must always and only be done to pursue the mission of the church.[1]

In this chapter, I will point out a few property-related matters that I believe are especially pertinent for parishes and their pastors. Bear in mind that most dioceses will undoubtedly have specific policies and procedures pertaining to the acquisition and alienation of property, especially real property. These points should be read in light of those local policies.

The first point is that one ought to find out exactly what the diocesan policies and procedures are for real property (land and buildings, real estate) in the diocese. Having that information, a pastor needs to take the time to work with both his pastoral and finance councils, perhaps even with some kind of special planning body, to determine what the long-term needs of the parish are. Looking down the road, what can we tell about our membership, the worship, education, and social space that will be needed in the future? Here, again, good hard data is critical. Perhaps this is most important when there is a question of selling contiguous land.

I was once the pastor of a small quasiparish that became a parish after a few years as the population grew. The problem was that we were in need of land on which to build a parish social center and ultimately a new church. As I discussed our need with the parish, some of the elders told me that, years before, the parish had owned a huge tract of land that was contiguous with its current property. That old tract extended all the way down to a scenic river, probably a quarter of a mile down the road! The parish had sold all that contiguous land years ago, and no one could remember exactly what the reasons were. In my tearful mind's eye, I could see a nice social center with a patio overlooking the river. What might have been!

The upshot is to be wary about selling contiguous property. The parish may have immediate financial needs, but too often the sale of property becomes the easiest path to solve those immediate needs, instead of the hard work of a capital campaign or an offertory increase campaign. It may be that contiguous property needs to be sold, but the parish, to my mind, should be hesitant, because fifty years in the future the parish may indeed need the property for the mission of the parish.

When it comes to buying property, there is also a need for practical data. I had a simple rule of thumb when purchasing property: Walk the land personally prior to buying it. That walk gives you information you cannot get any other way. I once looked at property for a parish church. When I actually went out and walked the entire plot, it was clear to me that we would not be able to use a significant portion of it because of environmental issues with drainage and wetland. There would also be questions of access and egress from the busy street in front of the property. I could not have known the extent of the potential problems from simply looking at a picture or seeing the property from the road. The result was a list of questions I had for my advisors. We finally decided that the up-front costs of dealing with the environmental and traffic issues would exhaust our resources even before we got to the point of planning and constructing a new church building on the land.

There have also been occasions when, before the end of the calendar year, someone approaches the parish with an offer to donate property. Yes, people are often generous and a diocese or parish can benefit greatly from such generosity. However, it is also true that people from time to time find themselves in positions that make it expedient for them to give their problem property away to charity for their own financial benefit.

It is important to do some research before accepting a property donation. The diocese should be brought into the discussion. There are a number of questions that should be asked:

Is the land useable by the parish?

Have toxic materials ever been used, produced, or stored on the land?

Is the land saleable, if that is intended by the parish?

Is the investment of time and resources to accept the land worth it?

It is always tempting when someone comes to you as the pastor and says he or she has property to give the parish. But the appropriate questions need to be asked with advisors. My advice: Be grateful for such offers, but take time to do research and to think through your response.

When assigned to a new parish, especially with a large parcel of land, I would again recommend that the new pastor take the time to walk the property. I remember in a suburban parish where I was pastor, I found a well with only a large piece of plywood over it. This was a safety hazard in spades, with neighborhood children running across the property at various times.

I also think it is important to introduce oneself to the neighbors when arriving as the new pastor. Building a cordial relationship with neighbors is another pastorally smart thing to do. If neighbors are not Catholic, such acts of reaching across the fence are a kind of evangelization. I would want to know their past experience with the parish and its activities. Neighbors may have had problems with noise or parking or some other things, and if those can be ironed out, it makes a lot of common sense. It is a good way to start your ministry of reconciliation!

Sometimes a parish church and a neighbor have unwritten agreements about shared use or permission to use a specific piece of property. Just as one would with a lease or a rental agreement, it is always the case that those permissions or shared-use verbal agreements should be put into writing so that there is no misunderstanding. Otherwise, I can think of a number of situations where unforeseen problems might arise. For example, suppose a parish has a van that it uses for seniors and youth, and there is a simple verbal agreement with the neighbor to park the van on his property. Or suppose the use of the neighbor's property was never really sought, but presumed. What happens if the van is vandalized? Where are the lines of responsibility? It is prudent to have those kinds of agreements in writing where possible. At least, it can help stave off hurt feelings or embarrassment on either side. At one downtown parish where I served, we allowed the school across the street to use our parking lot during the week. As I recall, there was no written agreement. The first thing the staff asked me to do when I became pastor was to draw up a formal written agreement between the church and the school in order to avoid any future misunderstandings.

B. Maintenance and Building Needs

The best lesson I ever learned as a pastor, when it came to maintenance and facilities needs, is the need to have a plan to care for the buildings. While members of the staff and the finance council actually did the administrative tasks involved, I made sure we had a *program* for preventative maintenance.

No matter how large your "plant," when you consider the amount of ordinary use the church and other buildings get, it seems only prudent that there be a schedule of care. To me this is a kind of stewardship. As it happens, though, it seems far too many of us live in a crisis mode when it comes to upkeep of buildings.

I have found that one doesn't have to reinvent the wheel to devise a maintenance plan. There are a number of helpful organizations and web sites that will provide you with a checklist for everything from masonry walls outside to floor finishes and fixtures on the inside.[2]

When maintenance is neglected, it can not only lead to a sudden problem, but it can also become a dangerous and expensive predicament. In the first parish I was assigned to, the boiler that heated the church and the school set off an alarm indicating it was reaching a very dangerous temperature and pressure. The fire department came and diffused the immediate danger, but I can remember one of the firemen asking the pastor if the ducts that carried the warm air to the various rooms had ever been cleaned. The church and school were at least twenty years old at that time. The pastor said they had never been cleaned. It seems the boiler was laboring mightily to force hot air through ducts that were pretty clogged with debris. What came out was not warm air, but lots of black sooty smoke. The building had to be cleaned and repainted.

Along these lines, I would raise a caution flag on allowing people in the parish who are not professionally qualified to do certain kinds of maintenance. I am thinking particularly of electrical work. People will offer to save the parish money by offering to do work at no cost. I am all for that, if only to encourage stewardship. However, there are limits. Here, again, without the proper experience, dangerous situations can arise, such as fire, not to mention the legal problems if the appropriate permits and inspections are neglected. The prudent and safe way to proceed in this area is to use qualified workers.

Questions for Discussion

1. How would you plan for the long-term use of parish land and buildings?
2. What kinds of things in the parish offices and church require a schedule of regular maintenance?
3. What kinds of situations do you think would cause a parish or diocese not to accept a gift of real estate?
4. "Any time property that is contiguous to the parish comes on the market, it is usually wise to buy it, if at all possible." Do you agree?
5. Volunteers can help with property maintenance. What tasks would you allow a volunteer to do, and what tasks would you not allow a volunteer to do? What about the age of the volunteer?

CHAPTER SIX

Insurance and Risk Management

A. Insurance

If you do an Internet search for "types of insurance," you will find that there are some 150 different kinds of insurance to cover almost any conceivable need. All insurance is, of course, a kind of hedge against some kind of loss. When it comes to coverage for parishes, each diocese has its own particular way of responding to the need to cover losses.

In general parishes will require *property insurance*. This coverage ordinarily insures the parish buildings and their contents against such things as fire, theft, weather damage, vandalism, and, in some cases, earthquake. Undoubtedly, dioceses will cover a priest's personal property, setting some dollar limit on a building, such as the parish rectory, that is also covered by the diocese's property insurance. This is another one of those times when each priest ought to talk to the people in the diocesan office to find out whether and to what extent his possessions are covered in a diocesan location. With all the technology that is available, not to mention clothing, books, hobby materials, etcetera, it seems only prudent to know whether all one's personal property would be covered if there were, say, a fire in the rectory. With this information, a priest can decide whether he wants to pursue additional separate coverage or not.

Dioceses usually have some form of general *liability insurance* as well. Simply stated, liability insurance is insurance that covers a legal claim made against the insured. These kinds of claims arise from operating the church and the school, and usually it involves some injury, such as slips and falls on parish property. A word of caution: If you have a dog or other pet, you might want to be sure that any loss or damage arising from the animal's behavior would be covered by either the diocesan insurance or your own coverage, if you have it. I recall a situation in which the pastor's usually affable little dog was frightened by the actions of a child in the rectory and nipped the child. Needless to say, damages were claimed.

When it comes to *auto insurance*, each diocese will have its own approach. Some dioceses will insure the priests' cars and all parish vehicles. Other dioceses will have each priest insure his own car, but will insure parish vehicles. Whatever turns out to be the case, the priest ought to be aware of the limits of his own coverage, as well as that of the parish vehicles. Remember, auto insurance simply involves paying a premium, and in return the insurer agrees to cover any loss according to the policy you have for damage or theft of your car, the liability you may incur for property damage or bodily injury, and medical costs for any injuries.

Another area that deserves mention is the area of what I will call *special events*. There are few parishes that do not have some kind of social space: a hall, a gym, a school cafeteria. That social space is often rented by parishioners and nonparishioners alike for nonparish events, such as large family gatherings. These kinds of events, especially when they are not directly parish-related, should raise a caution flag, especially if alcohol is going to be served. In order to protect the parish and the diocese from an unforeseen bad situation that might arise, many dioceses offer some kind of special-events insurance. Usually for a small price, appropriate coverage can be purchased to cover the event.

My experience as vicar for finance taught me that many pastors did not fully understand how diocesan property and liability insurance operated. Most assumed that were there to be a claim, say a fire or wind damage to the church, the insurance from the diocese that the parish paid for regularly would simply pay for all the damage. The notion was that, after a small deductible, some insurance company was going to pay for all the damage. They saw our insurance similar to their auto insurance, wherein they have, for example, a $200 deductible, and then the repairs are made and the insurance company picks up the bill. That is partially true.

As it happens, the insurance situation of many dioceses involves something referred to as *self-insurance*. That means that the archdiocese is virtually its own insurance company for the first x amount of dollars. Only on claims that are above that x amount does the archdiocese have what is called *reinsurance* purchased from an outside company. This upper level of insurance gives protection against unexpected terrible losses. Importantly, when the diocese purchases reinsurance at an upper level, that should, in theory, make the purchase of outside insurance less expensive than purchasing insurance that covers the same kinds of events from the very first dollar or with a modest deductible.

I raise all this, even though it may seem a bit complex or unimportant, for a purpose. In those dioceses that are self-insured, the fewer claims there are on the first layer or deductible (what is called the *self-insured retention* or SIR) the lower the cost to parishes. Remember, the parishes are their own insurance for that first layer up to x dollars. The way to make sure there are few claims on the SIR and thus on all the parishes that pay into the diocesan insurance program is to monitor carefully the risks that are out there.

B. Risk Management

If parishes and their staff members monitor the various risks that are inherent in operating the parish, then the need to make a claim should obviously be reduced. For example, making sure stairwells are well lit or that there are handrails for the elderly, means there is less risk that someone will fall down the church steps.

Every year around Advent and Lent, churches tend to hang special decorations and wreaths with candles in the worship space, and sometimes those items are rather large and are hung from rafters and other hard-to-reach places. One would be surprised at the things people stand on to do the hanging! This is another instance where using an ounce of prevention is much better than needing a pound of cure. This is also true in schools, where teachers have been known to stand on a chair placed on a student desk, only to have the chair slide off the desk. The reality is, with a little oversight, these kinds of accidents can be prevented. The variations on this theme are almost endless, but the wise pastor will be mindful of them not only because he wants his people and staff to be safe when they use parish facilities, but also because he wants to do his part to keep the insurance costs to *all* the parishes down.

One way to stay on top of the risk management in the parish is, first, to become familiar with the diocesan documents that address it. Second, start each parish staff meeting with a moment that allows the staff to mention anything that is a physical risk and needs to be checked by the parish maintenance person. This is a small thing in the scope of parish life, but it is not unimportant for the safety of people and the stewardship of church monies.

I am *not* advocating that the pastor or someone else go around in some kind of policing action. Not at all. What I am advocating is a "Safety first!" mindset among the entire parish staff, since they are the ones on the frontlines of parish life. If the pastor and staff can simply review parish activities, especially activities such as child care, use of vehicles, use of facilities for fund raisers, receptions, retreats, family reunions, *quinceañeras*, and the like, that will go a long way in helping to prevent accidents and other problems. I would also recommend that someone in the parish (perhaps a knowledgeable person from the finance and administrative council) be given the task of regularly assessing for risk. At the same time, it would also be helpful to inventory the parish's property. There are plenty of helpful checklists out there for this purpose, as well as the possibility of videoing the contents of the parish offices and the church and even the rectory and school.

Finally, whatever guidelines either the diocese or the parish establishes for eliminating or reducing risks need to be known, not only by the full-time staff, but also by part-time staff and volunteers.

Questions for Discussion

1. Is your diocese self-insured, or does it purchase coverage elsewhere?
2. Does your diocese cover your personal possessions from fire and theft if you live in the parish rectory? If yes, what are the limits of the coverage?
3. As a parish priest, what kind of risks would be present were you to organize a trip for your youth group to travel by van to a youth rally in a neighboring state?
4. Hypothetically, were there no insurance coverage available at all for your parish, how would you approach prevention problems?
5. As a pastor, how would you be sure your volunteers and staff were not taking unnecessary risks themselves in their work and were not subjecting parishioners, especially children, to risk?

CHAPTER SEVEN

Administration of Sacraments

Over the years, I have noticed that when pastors get together to socialize, one of the topics that inevitably comes up that generates some heated discussions is the administration of the sacraments, especially weddings, baptisms, and events such as *quinceañeras* (coming-of-age celebrations for teenage girls in Spanish-speaking cultures). These celebrations are often a source of frustration for pastors. This is not surprising to me. These occasions are highly emotional for families and individuals. Part of the reason for this, it seems to me, is that the popular culture tends to dictate so much of what people have their hearts set on for the liturgy before they even get to the church or talk to the pastor about how the Catholic Church celebrates these occasions. Pastors want the particular occasion firstly to be about faith and Church, as well as to incorporate the special touches people want, when appropriate. Pastors often anxiously discuss how to accomplish this goal.

I have found Father Ron Lewinski's book *Making Parish Policy: A Workbook on Sacramental Policies* to be helpful as a response to many, if not most, of the concerns that pastors have with respect to administering sacraments. In the book, Father Lewinski discusses the importance of having well-thought-out policies and procedures for the sacraments that are routinely celebrated in the parish. Father Lewinski notes that "the universal church has basic laws that govern sacramental practice….The diocesan bishop also has the authority to issue specific liturgical laws for the diocesan church as long as they do not contradict the universal law….At the parish level, the pastor may issue policies that are mandatory for the parish, provided these policies are in accord with universal and diocesan law (canon 519)."[1] It is having these policies and procedures at the parish level that I have found go a long way in resolving issues around the administration of sacraments.

Here again, we need to see the matter as one of building and sustaining relationships. We want the sacraments to draw people into a deeper relationship with their parish church and thus into a deeper relationship with the risen Lord. Reasonable policy can promote this.

Every pastor has a wedding-liturgy-preparation-gone-awry story. The couple expects one thing, and the pastor wants something else. Often what the couple requests is not in the marriage ritual, or for some other reason may not be liturgically appropriate. In some cases, the couple saw something at a civil or other non-Catholic wedding and they would like the priest to do the same thing. This kind of tension can usually be greatly diffused from the start by having a set of policies and procedures that are sent to the couple when they first call for an appointment. In this day and age, when e-mailing with attachments is so common, it is not difficult to welcome the prospect of the couple's wedding when the first phone call is received, and then to send a welcoming e-mail with a copy of the parish wedding policy that covers all the necessary aspects of the liturgy. I have found that couples who are presumably more interested in some other rites, rather than the Church's rites as described in the parish policies, do not pursue the matter.

I want to be clear that, as Father Lewinski points out, parish sacramental policies should *not* be the result of a pastor's anger over some negative experience from the past, for example, over a wedding where there was considerable tension from conflicting expectations. What preestablished policies can and will do for pastors and other church workers is provide a basis for making decisions that are equitable and fair. They can also be publicized in the parish so that people can come to rely on them. As Father Lewinski again points out, the policies are for the purpose of a healthy sacramental life in the parish.[2] In saying this, I am not advocating some rigid approach to celebrating sacraments. Parish policies need to be reasonable and responsible.

I have found that drafting policies with the parish pastoral council and asking several diocesan offices (for example, worship, judicial affairs, even family life) to review the policies for accuracy with respect to universal and diocesan norms is important. Again, by emphasizing policies and procedures, I am not trying to exclude anyone from celebrating the sacraments of the Catholic Church. On the contrary, I am hoping to safeguard the Catholic nature of the sacraments by being aware of elements that are not of our tradition and that would not draw people into the mystery of God.[3]

When administering the sacraments, be sure that the people involved have access to all the necessary information. For example, whenever the parish decides to celebrate baptisms, whether at Mass or at another time, that information should be available to the parish on a constant basis, for example in the Sunday bulletin or on the parish web site. In several parishes where I was pastor, the annual calendar would be set with the dates and times that baptism would be celebrated. It happened that we celebrated baptism at Mass six times a year. Those Sundays were advertised all year long so that people could plan ahead for family travel and the like. Baptism was also celebrated at unscheduled times as the need arose, but the established times were well known.

In chapter 1 I said that parish administration should be seen as St. Paul describes it: ministry. If a pastor can have a ministry mindset toward the administration of sacraments, it will help him to be attentive to recording the celebration of baptisms, marriages, and the deaths or funerals of parishioners. Admittedly, the paperwork and recording of sacramental occasions is not the most exciting work one could imagine; nevertheless, the responsibility for the proper recording of sacraments is the pastor's. He can delegate it to the parish secretary or some other reliable person, but he is still responsible.

I emphasize this matter because there truly is a certain justice involved. Since a baptismal certificate can be used as proof of age for various civil documents or even be used in civil litigation, there is a moral obligation, it seems to me, to keep these records accurately and conscientiously. I would include in "conscientiously" that records need to be kept in a way that protects them from being destroyed. A pastor recently told me that he once inadvertently stored parish sacramental, historical, and financial records in the church basement under a water pipe. The pipe froze in the winter and then broke and destroyed all the records that were below it! Included in the mess were photos from years past that would have been invaluable for future generations.[4]

Questions for Discussion

1. Parish policies may either be written out or unstated. What are some examples of unwritten policies operating in many parishes?
2. If you were pastor, what written policies would you implement for baptism, marriage, first communion? How did you arrive at your policies?
3. Is it possible to be overly restrictive in providing sacraments for your parishioners? What would be some examples?
4. What sacramental records does the Church require parishes to keep?
5. In some parishes, anyone who receives a sacrament is "automatically" registered as a parishioner. Do you agree with that policy?

CHAPTER EIGHT
A Final Word on Relationships

I began this work by describing the communion of local churches that goes to the heart of the Catholic Church. I pointed out that the relationship of local churches with one another and with the bishop of Rome is the key to understanding our catholicity. I further pointed out that the bishop of the local church, as a pastor, has a relationship with his priests and people, and that relationship is at the heart of the diocese. Finally, I pointed out that the pastor of the parish is likewise to have a relationship with his people in order to bring about the communion of the parish with him, with one another, and with the larger church. These are the fundamental relationships that are the Catholic Church's structure, and they go to the very nature of what the Church is: a communion of the baptized here below that mirrors the communion of saints above.

Having said all that, I want to speak a bit more about the pastor as the shepherd of parish relationships. These are the basic building blocks of our Church, and the parish pastor is a primary builder of those foundational relationships that make the parish and the larger church a communion. It cannot be stated too strongly how important for administering a parish this axiom is. It is also why administration should be seen as ministry. I want to point out that parish administration as such does not so much create parish relationships as it fosters, develops, maintains, supports, and directs those relationships. No minor feat! To accomplish those tasks with all the attention they require takes a mature leader, one who clearly is "relational."

The "bible" for priestly formation in our seminaries is the *Program of Priestly Formation*. In it, the bishops of the United States speak of the need of a future priest to be "a person who has real and deep relational capacities, someone who can enter into genuine dialogue and friendship, a person of true empathy who can understand and know other persons, a person open to others and available to them with a generosity of spirit…." And elsewhere they state that a future priest needs to be able (or learn the skills to be able) to "relate well with others, free of overt prejudice and willing to work with people of diverse cultural backgrounds: a man capable of wholesome relationships with women and men as relatives, friends, colleagues, staff members, and teachers…."[1]

As I read those texts, I hear the bishops acknowledging that the key to the pastor-parish relationship and administration is personal maturity. Indeed, in many of the examples of behavior mentioned in this book, it was the pastor's maturity that was the focus to my mind. To be sure, there is always room for emotional growth in all our lives. Long ago, I had a seminary professor who once told us students that the "whole struggle of life is to get out of adolescence!" There is much truth in that. But being the pastor and the leader and administering the parish community demands a certain level of personal maturity beyond adolescence. Without it, various kinds of problems arise with staff, parishioners, and often the diocese. Someone has said that "immaturity that isn't transformed is transmitted." The problem for the parish with an immature leader is that the community is harmed, even fractured, and at its worst, there is a loss of communion.

What do I mean by the maturity needed for pastoral administration of a parish by a priest? First, I would say the priest needs self-insight. He must be aware of his strengths and weaknesses and be able to articulate them. He ought to be able to "own" his own life and take responsibility for it, as well as for his decisions, accepting both affirmation and constructive criticism. Next, I would say he needs to be able to make prudent decisions and be able to follow through with his decisions. In decision making, being able to say *no* is every bit as important as being able to say *yes*. This means that a good pastoral administrator needs to be appropriately assertive, while always respecting others. Thirdly, I would stress that maturity includes the ability of a pastor to forgo his own preferences for the sake of the good of the whole parish. Next, I would say again what I have emphasized throughout these pages: The mature administrator knows when to ask for help.[2]

In sum, there is no substitute for the relationship-building power of a pastor who is a mature leader. As I read and reread the Gospels, I find Jesus' respect and compassion for people, his ability to relate to rich and poor, women and men, young and old, followers and nonfollowers alike as evidence of his personal maturity. It is that same Jesus that we are called to follow and imitate as pastors and parish administrators. It is what our people look for and instinctively recognize. It is what they really expect and deserve. With mature leadership, the parish can advance steadily toward the fulfillment of its mission, and the Church, the community, and even the world are all better for it.

Questions for Discussion

1. What are some ways besides liturgical practices that bishops exercise their pastoral role for their local church?
2. What do you understand by being a "relational" pastor and "pastoring is all about relationships"? What might be some behaviors that you would like to find in your pastor if you were a layperson?
3. What is meant by "immaturity that isn't transformed is transmitted"?
4. What does it mean to "own" your own life?
5. What personal skills does it take to forgo one's own preferences for the sake of the whole parish? What spiritual insight might make it easier?

Notes

CHAPTER ONE

1. *The Code of Canon Law* (Grand Rapids, MI: William Eerdmans, 1983), c. 368.

2. *The Rites II* (New York: Pueblo Publishing, 1976), 67.

3. "2004–5 Diocesan Staff Salary Survey," *CARA Report* 11 (2005):11.

4. *Presbyterorum Ordinis* in *The Documents of Vatican II*, ed. Walter M. Abbot, SJ (New York: Guild Press, 1966), §43, p. 539.

5. Louis W. Bloede, *The Effective Pastor: A Guide to Successful Ministry* (Minneapolis, MN: Augsburg Fortress Press, 1966), 67.

6. Pope John Paul II, *I Will Give You Shepherds: On the Formation of Priests in the Circumstances of the Present Day* (Washington, DC: USCC, 1992), 118.

7. Anonymous Parishioner, "Our Broken Parish," *America* 198 (2008): 24–25.

8. Ibid.

9. Marti Jewell and David Ramsey, "Marks of Pastoral Excellence: Some More Difficult than Others," *Sustaining Pastoral Excellence Newsletter* (September, 2005): 1–4.

10. *Parish Pastoral Planning* (Portland, OR: Archdiocese of Portland, 1999), 5–8.

11. *The Code of Canon Law*, c. 547.

CHAPTER TWO

1. Richard B. Couser, *Ministry and the American Legal System* (Minneapolis, MN: Augsburg Fortress Press, 1993), 65.

2. Ibid., 65–66.

CHAPTER THREE

1. Richard B. Couser, *Ministry and the American Legal System* (Minneapolis, MN: Augsburg Fortress Press, 1993), 110.

CHAPTER FOUR

1. *The Code of Canon Law* (Grand Rapids, MI: William Eerdmans, 1983), c. 1284.

2. Wayne Martin Lenel, *Income Taxes for Priests Only* (Chicago: National Federation of Priests' Councils, 2007), 67.

CHAPTER FIVE

1. "The Temporal Goods of the Church," in *The Code of Canon Law* (Grand Rapids, MI: William Eerdmans, 1983), 220–29.

2. I have found architect Michael Borskie's *Many Values— Many Voices* newsletter to be useful. In vol. 2008, no. 2, I found a wonderful checklist for a maintenance inspection program. The program helps one make facilities evaluations according to what needs to happen monthly, twice yearly, and annually.

CHAPTER SEVEN

1. Ron Lewinski, *Making Parish Policy: A Workbook on Sacramental Policies* (Chicago: Liturgical Training Press, 1996), 4.

2. Ibid., 5.

3. Ibid., 6.

4. See also *The Code of Canon Law* (Grand Rapids, MI: William Eerdmans, 1983), c. 535, nos. 1–5.

CHAPTER EIGHT

1. *Program of Priestly Formation*, 5th ed. (Washington, DC: USCC, 2006), 30–31.

2. *Dimensions for Evaluations* (St. Benedict, OR: Mount Angel Seminary, 2007), 4.